Like the bee
gathering honey from
the different flowers,
the wise person
accepts the
essence
of the
different
scriptures
and sees
only
the good
in all
religions.

M.K.Gandhi

Mahatma Gandhi

The Golden Rule

There is a Golden Thread that weaves the
prayers, blessings and sacred verses of all of
the Prophets of God from all the religions together...

HINDUISM — Do not to others what ye do not wish done to yourself, and wish for others what ye desire and long for for yourself.

JUDAISM — Thou shalt love thy neighbor as thyself.

ZOROASTRIAN — Whatever is disagreeable to you, do not do unto others.

BUDDHISM — Hurt not others in ways that you yourself would find hurtful.

CHRISTIANITY — Do unto others as you would have them do unto you.

ISLAM — None of you truly believes until he wishes for his brother what he wishes for himself.

BAHÁÍ — And if thine eyes be turned towards justice, choose thou for thy neighbor that which thou choosest for thyself.

O God,

O God,
guide me, protect me,
make of me a shining
lamp and a brilliant star.
Thou art the Mighty
and the Powerful.

'Abdu'l-Bahá

Bem aventurado é o lugar,
a casa e o caroção,
e bem aventurada a cidade,
a montanha, o refúgio,
a caverna e o vale, a terra e o mar,
o prado e a ilha, onde se haja feito
menção de Deus e celebrado Seu Louvor.

Portuguese

Geseënd is de plek, en die huis,
en die plaas, en die stad,
en die hart, en die berg,
en die toevlug, en die grot,
en die vallei, en die land,
en die see, en die eiland,
en die weiveld waar melding van God
gemaak is, en Sy lof verheerlik is.

Afrikaans

Bahá'u'lláh

Blessed
is the spot,
and the house,
and the place,
and the city,
and the heart,
and the mountain,
and the refuge,
and the cave,
and the valley,
and the land,
and the sea,
and the island,
and the meadow,
where mention of God hath been made and His praise glorified.

Bahá'u'lláh

Love is patient,
love is kind and
envies no one.
Love is never boastful
nor conceited, nor rude,
never selfish, not quick
to take offense.
Love keeps no score
of wrongs, does not
gloat over other men's
sins, but delights in
the truth.
There is nothing love
cannot face and there
is no limit to its faith,
hope and its endurance.
Love will never come
to an end. There are three
things that last forever -
faith, hope and love.
But the greatest one of
all is love.

The Bible

Christianity

Our Father who art in heaven,
hallowed be Thy name.
Thy kingdom come,
Thy will be done,
on earth as it is in heaven.

Give us this day our daily bread
and forgive us our trespasses,
as we forgive them that trespass
against us, and lead us
not into temptation
but deliver us from evil.

For thine is the kingdom,
and the power, and the glory
for ever and ever.
Amen.

✝

A cross is a symbol
of Christianity.
It represents the
sacrifice and
resurrection of
Jesus Christ.

From the Bible

O, ANGEL OF GOD, MY GUARDIAN DEAR,
TO WHOM GOD'S LOVE COMMITS ME HERE,
EVER THIS NIGHT BE AT MY SIDE,
TO LIGHT AND GUARD,
TO RULE AND GUIDE ME.
AMEN. CHRISTIAN

He is God! O God, my God!
Bestow upon me a pure heart, like unto a pearl.

彼こそは神におわします。おお、神さま、私の神さま。私に、真珠のように清らかな心をお与えください。 *Bahá'i*

Japanese

Bedtime
Blessings

Sweet dreams.

Que sueñes con los angelitos.

O Lord,
Grant that this night we may sleep in peace.
And that in the morning our awakening may also be peace.
May our daytime be cloaked in your peace. Protect us and
inspire us to think and act only out of love. Keep far from
us all evil; may our paths be free from all obstacles from
when we go out until we return home. Jewish blessing

Now I lay me down to sleep,
I pray the Lord my soul to keep.
May God guard me through the night
And wake me with the morning light. Christian

My mind can go in a thousand directions.
Now I walk in peace.
Each step creates a warm breeze.
With each step, a lotus blooms. Buddhist

Blessed are the children who have hope, for it is life's
joyous gift from the Great Mystery. When I sleep
I pray to the Great Mystery, whom I love, that I
bond to that part of life which is eternal.
All my relations! Lakota/Sioux

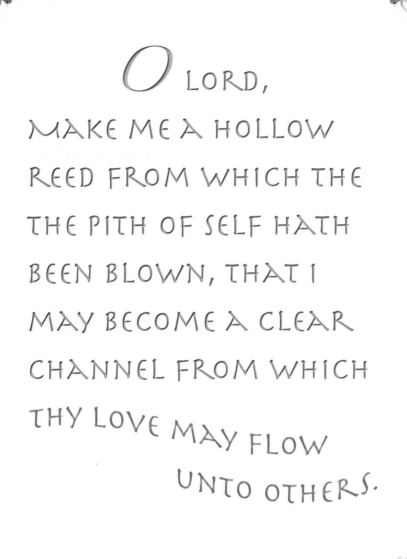

O LORD,
MAKE ME A HOLLOW
REED FROM WHICH THE
THE PITH OF SELF HATH
BEEN BLOWN, THAT I
MAY BECOME A CLEAR
CHANNEL FROM WHICH
THY LOVE MAY FLOW
UNTO OTHERS.

GEORGE TOWNSHEND, BAHÁ'Í AUTHOR

Giving Thanks

For food in a world where many walk in hunger. For friends in a world where many walk alone. For faith in a world where many walk in fear. We give You Thanks, O Lord. Amen.

Anglican

Brahmaarpanam, Brahma Havir Brahmaagnau Brahmanaa Hutam Brahmaiva Tena Gantavyam Brahma Karma Samaadhinaha The act of offering is God (Brahma), the oblation is God, by God it is offered into the fire of God, God is That which is to be attained by him who sees God in all. Hindu

Make us worthy, Lord, to serve those people throughout the world who live and die in poverty and hunger. Give them through our hand this day their daily bread, and by our understanding love, give peace and joy. Mother Teresa

Bless us O Lord and these Thy gifts which we are about to receive from Thy bounty through Christ, our Lord. Amen.

Catholic

We thank Great Spirit for the resources that made this food possible; we thank the Earth Mother for producing it, and we thank all those who labored to bring it to us. May the Wholesomeness of the food before us, bring out the Wholeness of the Spirit within us. *Native American*

Mealtime Blessings

I take this nourishment in gratitude (to all beings). Thank you in deepest gratitude (to sustain my life).

Buddhist Blessing

Thank you, Oh Allah, for feeding us and making us amongst the believers.

Islamic

Mother Earth, Mother Earth, Take thy seed and give it birth, Father Sun, gleam and glow, Until the root begins to grow, Sister Rain, Sister Rain, Shed thy tear to swell the grain.

Waldorf

He is God! Thou seest us, O my God, gathered around this table, praising Thy bounty, with our gaze set upon Thy Kingdom. O Lord! Send down upon us Thy heavenly food and confer upon us Thy blessing. Thou art verily the Bestower, the Merciful, the Compassionate. *Bahá'i Faith*

Jewish blessing:

BLESSED ART THOU, CREATOR OF THE UNIVERSE, WHO BRINGS FORTH FOOD FROM THE EARTH.

a home for the stranger

generous

a treasure
to the
poor

thankful

eyes
to
the
blind

guided

fair

a tower
of strength

a lamp
in darkness

a breath of life

a guiding light

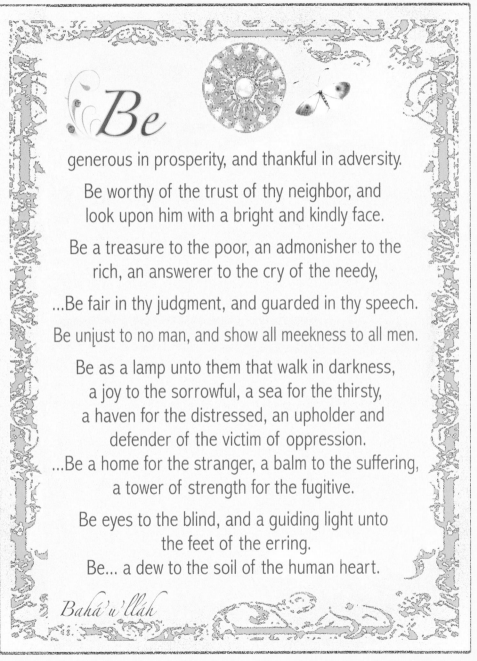

Be generous in prosperity, and thankful in adversity.

Be worthy of the trust of thy neighbor, and
look upon him with a bright and kindly face.

Be a treasure to the poor, an admonisher to the
rich, an answerer to the cry of the needy,

...Be fair in thy judgment, and guarded in thy speech.

Be unjust to no man, and show all meekness to all men.

Be as a lamp unto them that walk in darkness,
a joy to the sorrowful, a sea for the thirsty,
a haven for the distressed, an upholder and
defender of the victim of oppression.

...Be a home for the stranger, a balm to the suffering,
a tower of strength for the fugitive.

Be eyes to the blind, and a guiding light unto
the feet of the erring.

Be... a dew to the soil of the human heart.

Bahá'u'lláh

defender

fair

guarded
in thy
speech

a haven
for the
distressed

a sea for
the thirsty

a
bright
and
kindly
face

佑
protect

和睦
harmony

爱
love

仁慈
kindness

文雅
gentleness

Buddhism

和平
peace

We will be kind and gentle
to every living thing
and protect all who are
weaker than ourselves.

We will think pure
and beautiful thoughts,
say pure and beautiful words,
and do pure and beautiful deeds.

Buddhist Prayer

The Wheel of Dhamma
symbol represents the
continuous cycle of
birth, life and death
of a Buddhist.

Er nokkur sá er
firrir erfiðleikum
nema Guð?
Seg: lof sé Guði,
Hann er Guð!
Allir eru þjónar
Hans og allir lúta
boðum Hans.

Icelandic

¿Quién libra de
las dificultades
salvo Dios?
Di: ¡Alabado
sea Dios!
¡Él es Dios!
Todos somos sus
siervos y todos
nos atenemos a
su mandato.

Spanish

Is there
any Remover
of difficulties,
save God?
Say: Praised
be God!
He is God!
All are His
servants,
and
all abide
by His
bidding!

The Báb

"May you be blessed with the strength of heaven,
the light of the sun and the radiance of the moon,
the splendor of fire, the speed of lightning,
the swiftness of wind, the depth of the sea,
the stability of earth, and the firmness of rock."
St. Patrick's Blessing

"Every blade of grass has its angel that bends over it and whispers,
'Grow. Grow.'" The Talmud

"Be strong as a panther, light as an eagle, swift as a gazelle, and bold as a lion
to carry out the will of your Father in Heaven.. " Jewish Baby Blessing

love you

Welcome to the world!

"May the sun bring you new energy by day.
May the moon softly restore you by night.
May the rain wash away your worries
And the breeze blow new strength into your being.
And all the days of your life may you walk
gently through the world and know its beauty."

An Apache Blessing

"You have come by the command of God. You have appeared to speak of Him. You were created to serve Him, the Dear, the Beloved."

Whispered into the ear of newborns
from an unknown Bahá'i source

Baby Blessings

"If you look deeply into the palm of your hand, you will see your parents and all generations of your ancestors. All of them are alive in this moment. Live well – you are a continuation of each of them."

A Vietnamese Baby Saying

dedicated to Pooran Abdi

From your *heart*

Alone,
with family or friends
with teachers
in congregation

Ways
people
pray

from a book or
from your memory
from your heart
meditate, hum, drum
play an instrument
twirl, dance, clap, sing
chant, out loud, silently
quietly, shout with joy
kneel down, stand, bow
lay down, walk about
sit up straight, sit
cross-legged, eyes
closed or open, look up
or down, look at nature
hands together, hands
apart, fingers crossed
or up or over your heart
arms up, out or crossed
with a good deed
with an act of service.

MAY ALL THE BEINGS
IN ALL THE WORLDS
BE HAPPY
MAY ALL THE BEINGS
IN ALL THE WORLDS
BE HAPPY.
MAY ALL THE BEINGS
IN ALL THE WORLDS
BE HAPPY.
OM, PEACE, PEACE, PEACE.

HINDU

Oh lord almighty, may there be peace in celestial regions. May there be peace on earth. May the waters be appeasing. May herbs be wholesome, and may trees and plants bring peace to all. May all beneficent beings bring peace to us... and may thy peace itself, bestow peace on all, and may that peace come to me also.

This symbol is the written form of the most sacred sound in Hinduism: aum or om. It represents the sound of God.

Prayers from the Hindu Faith

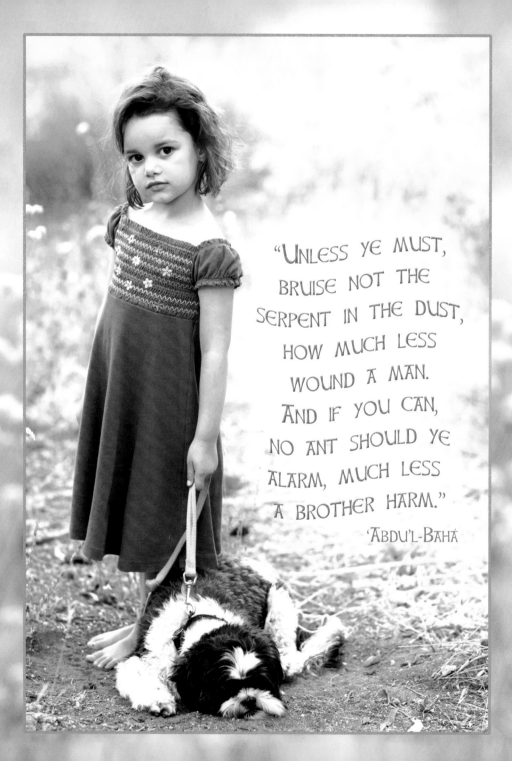

"Unless ye must,
bruise not the
serpent in the dust,
how much less
wound a man.
And if you can,
no ant should ye
alarm, much less
a brother harm."

'Abdu'l-Bahá

Train your children
from their earliest
days to be infinitely
tender and loving
to animals. If an
animal be sick, let
the children try to
heal it, if it be
hungry, let them
feed it, if thirsty
let them quench
its thirst, if weary
let them see
that it rests.

Bahá'í Faith

May all beings
everywhere plagued
with sufferings of bod
and mind quickly b
freed from their pair
May those frightene
cease to be afraid,
and may those boun
be free.
...May people
befriend all life.

Buddhist
Blessing

ANIMAL BLESSINGS

Blessed are you, Lord God, Maker of all living creatures. You inspired St. Francis to call all animals his brothers and sisters. We ask you to bless this animal. By the power of Your love enable it to live according to your plan. Amen.

Franciscan Pet Blessing

When I walk through Thy woods, may my right foot and my left foot be harmless to the little creatures that move in its grasses; as it is said by the mouth of thy prophet, they shall not hurt nor destroy in all my holy mountain.

A Rabbi's Blessing

O Lord, let my spirit glow

so brightly,

that darkness

will disappear.

The crescent moon
and star is a symbol
of the Islamic Faith.

ISLAM

Mohammed

O Lord, grant us to love Thee;

Grant that we may love those who love Thee;

Grant that we may do the deeds that win Thy love.

Make the love of Thee be dearer to us

than even ourselves, than our families, than

wealth, and even than cool water.

Mohammed

It is God who made the night for you, that you may rest therein,
and the day, as that which helps you to see. Verily, God is
full of grace and bounty to men, yet most men give no thanks.
It is God who has made you the earth as a resting place, and
the sky as a canopy, and has given you shape – and made your
shapes beautiful – and has provided for you sustenance of things
pure and good; such is God, your Lord. So glory to God, the
Lord of the Worlds!

Qur'án 40:61, 64

O Friend!
In the garden of
thy heart,
plant naught
but the rose
of love...

Ô ami!
Dans le jardin de
ton cœur, ne plante
que la rose d'amour...

French

朋友啊！

在你的心田里，
只种爱的玫瑰。
别让友爱与渴望之夜莺·
从你手中高飞。
珍视与正直者交谊，
切勿与邪恶者暧昧。

Chinese

Bahá'u'lláh

educate

trained

grow

&

develop

O God! Educate these children.
These children are the plants of Thine
orchard, the flowers of Thy meadow, the roses
of Thy garden. Let Thy rain fall upon them;
let the Sun of Reality shine upon them with
Thy love. Let Thy breeze refresh them in order
that they may be trained, grow and develop,
and appear in the utmost beauty. Thou art
the Giver. Thou art the Compassionate.

'Abdu'l-Bahá

O my God

صلات صغیر

و صلات اخریٰ حین زوال قرائت نماید :

اشهد یا الهی بانّك خلقتنی

لعرفانك و عبادتك

اشهد فی هٰذا الحین بعجزی و قوتك

و ضعفی و اقتدارك و فقری و غناۤئك

لا الٰه الّا انت المهیمن القیّوم

Arabic

I bear witness, O my God, that Thou hast created
me to know Thee and to worship Thee. I testify
at this moment, to my powerlessness and to
Thy might, to my poverty and to Thy wealth.
There is none other God but Thee, the
Help in Peril, the Self-Subsisting.

Noon day prayer

Bahá'u'lláh

Grandfather, Great Mystery, look this way
And all of the Directions To the Heavens above.
To the nurturing Mother Earth.
Purify this heart of mine
That my spirit expands forward
That my talk is towards the Great Mystery
Towards the sun I will stand beneath its light in joy
As the sacred child walks in its learning growth.
All My Relations.

Tunkasila, Wakan Tanka, ahetonwan yo makasitomni ya

Na magpya takiya na makoca takiya howayc.

Cante apo mayanyo ho hecel nagi mitawa ki

Tokatakiya yin kte

Wakan Tanka wowakiyakin kte

Wi oglata ajanjan wiyus kinyan nawajin ktc

Wakanyeja ki ecag ye waunspa ogna manipi.

Mitakuye Oyasin

Lakota language

Peter V. Catches
Lakota/Sioux, Medicine Man
Zintkala Oyate (Bird People)

Thy name is my healing, O my God, and remembrance of Thee is my remedy. Nearness to Thee is my hope, and love for Thee is my companion. Thy mercy to me is my healing and my succor in both this world and the world to come. Thou, verily art the All-Bountiful, the All-Knowing, the All-Wise.

On Ou se gerizon mwen, O Bon Dye, lè mwen sonje Ou, mwen jwenn remèd mwen. Vwazinai Ou se sèl espwa mwewn, lamou mwen pou Ou se konpayon mwen. Mizerikòd Ou se gerizon mwen ak soutyen mwen nan lemonn sa a ak lòt monn nan tou. An verite, Ou se Bon Dye ki gen tout bonte a, ki konnen toutbagav, ki gen tout sajès la.

- Hawaiian

Kou inoa ku'u ho'ōla, e ku'u Akua, a me ka ho'omana'o 'ana iā 'Oe ku'u lā'au. Kou alo ku'u mana'olana a me ke aloha Nou ku'u hoa like. Kou aloha ia'u ku'u ho̱ola a me ku'u maha i loko o ka honua a me ka honua o ka wā ma mua. 'O 'Oe ke Akua Ho'olako apau, ke Akua Ho̱'oia'i'o, ke Akua Ho'ona'auao apau.

- Haitian Creole

Bahá'u'lláh

If we
have no
peace, it is
because we have
forgotten that we
belong to each other.

Mother Teresa

O my God! O my God!

Unite the hearts of Thy servants, and reveal to them Thy great purpose. May they follow Thy commandments and abide in Thy law. Help them, O God, in their endeavor, and grant them strength to serve Thee. O God! Leave them not to themselves, but guide their steps by the light of Thy knowledge and cheer their hearts by Thy love. Verily, Thou art their Helper and their Lord.

Bahá'u'lláh

unite
the
hearts

cheer
their
hearts

guide
their
steps

A 9-pointed star is a symbol of the Bahá'í Faith. It signifies unity - the main principle of the followers of Bahá'u'lláh.

O Thou, Tz'aqol, B'itol!
Watch over us, hear us!
Do not leave us.
Do not leave us unsheltered,
Thou who art in Heaven,
and on Earth,
heart of the Heaven,
heart of the Earth!

Give us many good paths,
flat paths!
May the villages have peace!
Much peace to be happy and
give us a good and useful
existence!

From the Popol Wuj
Guatemalan Maya K'iche

Love, respect, compassion, strength, forgiveness, acceptance, trust

gratitude, consideration, dignity, generosity, kindness = PEACE

honesty, justice, understanding, tolerance, courage, courtesy

"There is no path to peace. Peace is the path."
Mahatma Gandhi

cooperation, patience, perseverance, service, unity, wisdom

O Thou kind Lord!
These lovely children are the handiwork
of the fingers of Thy might and
the wondrous signs of Thy greatness.
O God!

Protect these children, graciously assist
them to be educated and enable them to
render service to the world of humanity.
O God!

These children are pearls, cause them to
be nurtured within the shell
of Thy loving-kindness.
Thou art the Bountiful,
the All-Loving.

'Abdu'l-Bahá

¡O Tú, Dios bondadoso!
Estos niños encantadores
son obra de los dedos de
Tu poder y los signos
maravillosos de Tu
grandeza.

¡Oh, Dios!
Protege a
estos niños, ayúdales
bondadosamente a
cultivarse y capacítales
para prestar servicios
al mundo de la
humanidad.

¡Oh, Dios!
Estos niños
son perlas,
haz que se nutran
dentro de la concha de
Tu amorosa bondad.

Tú eres el Munífico
el Todo Amoroso.

Spanish

Judaism

The six points of
the star of David
represent the six
directions of God's
rule of the universe:
north, south, east
west, up and down.

May God bless you and
watch over you,
May God shine His
face toward you
and show you favor.
May God look on
you with favor and
grant you shalom peace.

Ye'varech'echa Adonoy
ve'yishmerecha.
Ya'ir Adonoy panav eilecha
viy-chuneka.
Yisa Adonoy panav eilecha,
ve'yasim lecha shalom.

יברכך יי
וישמרך
יאר יי פניו אליך ויחנך
ישא יי פניו אליך
וישם לך שלום

Hebrew

"EVERY BLADE OF GRASS HAS ITS ANGEL THAT BENDS OVER IT AND WHISPERS,
"GROW. GROW."
THE TALMUD

O LORD!

I AM A CHILD;
ENABLE ME TO GROW BENEATH
THE SHADOW OF THY LOVING-KINDNESS.

I AM A TENDER PLANT;
CAUSE ME TO BE NURTURED THROUGH THE
OUTPOURINGS OF THE CLOUDS OF THY BOUNTY.

I AM A SAPLING OF THE GARDEN OF LOVE;
MAKE ME INTO A FRUITFUL TREE.

THOU ART THE MIGHTY AND THE POWERFUL, AND THOU
ART THE ALL-LOVING, THE ALL-KNOWING, THE ALL-SEEING.

'Abdu'l-Bahá

O God!
Rear this little babe...

IN THE BOSOM OF THY LOVE...

O God! Rear this little babe in the bosom of Thy love, and give it milk from the breast of Thy Providence. Cultivate this fresh plant in the rose garden of Thy love and aid it to grow through the showers of Thy bounty. Make it a child of the kingdom, and lead it to Thy heavenly realm. Thou art powerful and kind, and Thou art the Bestower, the Generous, the Lord of surpassing bounty.

-'Abdu'l-Baha

This is a broken-winged bird...

O God! O God!
This is a broken-winged
bird and his flight is very slow -
assist him so that he may fly toward
the apex of prosperity and salvation,
wing his way with the utmost joy and
happiness throughout the illimitable
space, raise his melody in Thy Supreme
Name in all the regions, exhilarate the
ears with this call, and brighten the
eyes by beholding the signs of
guidance.

O Lord! I am single, alone and lowly.
For me their is no support save Thee,
no helper except Thee and no sustainer
beside Thee. Confirm me in Thy service, assist me with the cohorts of Thy angels,
make me victorious in the promotion of Thy Word and suffer me to speak out Thy
wisdom amongst Thy creatures. Verily, Thou art the helper of the weak and
the defender of the little ones, and verily Thou art the Powerful,
the Mighty and the Unconstrained.

'Abd'u'l-Bahá

O God!

Refresh and gladden my spirit. Purify my heart.
Illumine my powers. I lay all my affairs in Thy hand.
Thou art my Guide and my Refuge. I will no longer be
sorrowful and grieved; I will be a happy and joyful
being. O God! I will no longer be full of anxiety,
nor will I let trouble harrass me. I will not dwell
on the unpleasant things of life.

O God! Thou art more friend to me than I am to
myself. I dedicate myself to Thee, O Lord.

Bahá'í Faith, source unknown

Refresh and gladden my spirit

To consider that after the death
of the body the spirit perishes is
like imagining that a bird in a cage
will be destroyed if the cage is broken,
though the bird has nothing to fear
from the destruction of the cage.
Our body is like the cage, and the
spirit is like the bird. ...if the cage
becomes broken, the bird will
continue and exist. Its feelings will
be even more powerful, its perceptions
greater, and its happiness increased.
... for the thankful birds there is no
paradise greater than freedom from
the cage.

A Prayer for the Departed

O Lord, glorify his station, shelter him under the pavilion
of Thy supreme mercy, cause him to enter Thy glorious
paradise, and perpetuate his existence in Thine exalted
rose garden, that he may plunge into the sea of light in
the world of mysteries.

Abdu'l-Bahá

A Zoroastrian Prayer for Peace

We pray to God to eradicate all the misery in the world
that understanding triumph over ignorance,
that generosity triumph over indifference,
that trust triumph over contempt, and
that truth triumph over falsehood.

I worship You in every religion that teaches
Your laws and praises Your glory.

I worship You in every plant whose beauty
reflects Your beauty.

I worship You in every event which is caused
by Your goodness and kindness.

I worship You in every place You dwell.

And I worship You in every man and woman
who seeks to follow Your way
of righteousness.

Zoroastrian writing

The Zoroastrian Farohar
symbol has three layers
of feathers that stand
for good thoughts, good
words and good deeds.

My prayer

Thank you to all of the beautiful children for sharing these prayerful moments with us. Special thanks to Jenny Felimi Snook for your enchanting clothing design and styling.

This book is dedicated to a dear little friend, Kaeden McCarty, who at age five left this world unexpectedly for the next one. 2005-2011

Graphic design/art by Alice Williams
Photographs by Aimee Porter

Published by WorldBeat Productions, Calabasas, CA
Copyright © 2011 blessingsandgems.com

ISBN 978 0 615 43251 9
Printed by Gold Printing Group in China
www.goldprinting.cc

For more of our products: www.blessingsandgems.com
For more information about the Bahá'i Faith: www.bahai.org